TRADING STOCKS MADE EASY
HOW ANYONE CAN CREATE FINANCIAL FREEDOM IN THE STOCK MARKET

By Tyrone Jackson

www.TheWealthyInvestor.net

ISBN: 978-0972613712

First Edition

Dedication

To my lovely daughters
Danika and Makena
May all of your financial dreams
Become reality

Thank You

To Quinn Cassavale and Mark Phillips
for your dedication in
helping produce this work.

Table of Contents

About This Book

This book as designed to be a fast and easy introduction to the US Stock Market.

In ***Trading Stocks Made Easy***, my goal is to encourage you to seek the financial education you many not have received in High School or College. There is a world beyond paycheck to paycheck that is abundant behind your imagination.

Creating wealth and financial freedom for yourself has less to do with your higher education and has more to do with your financial education. Each and every day the richest people in the world generate profits of some kind in the stock market. Some do it through trading stocks, others through investing and dividend collection. With the right guidance and tutelage, you can do the same.

The stocks used in this book are not recommendations, but rather, illustrations of how your money would have grown had you been a shareholder of these very popular multinationals.

It's never to late to get started investing in stocks. These day's technological investments are diving profits on Wall Street. You will want to open an online trading account if you don't already have one. The next five years will very profitable and will create even more millionaires and billions than any other time in history.

Remember, you have the power to change your financial life. It all starts with the right financial education.

All my best!

Tyrone Jackson
The Wealthy Investor

About The Author

Tyrone Jackson, The Wealthy Investor, is a trusted stock market trader and teacher, who has built his reputation on his unique ability to simplify stock trading and investing. He is also a mentor and trusted wealth building coach to major Silicon Valley and Hollywood executives. A frequent guest on radio and TV shows, and a respected **Huffington Post** blogger, Tyrone educates his students on how to earn thousands of dollars each month as traders and investors.

Tyrone is the celebrated author of **"You Should Be Rich By Now: The Stock Market Trading and Investing Handbook"**, and **"Make Money Monthly Trading Stocks: Proven Tips & Strategies From a Successful Trader"**, both of which have been praised for their effectiveness in providing simple, proven ways to create wealth through online stock trading.

"My Wealthy Investor program is for those who want to change their lives by getting the education they didn't get in school," Tyrone says. "In today's world, to be successful you need a financial education."

Tyrone teaches how to choose stocks that have the highest probability of increasing in value. Best of all, his simple yet powerful system allows any investor to profit whether the market goes up, down, or stays the same.

You can visit his website at **www.TheWealthyInvestor.net** to learn more.

Change Your Financial Life

Why learn how to trade and invest in the stock market? The answer is simple: Over the last 100 years the stock market has consistently created more millionaires and billionaires than any other investment vehicle. In the mid 20th Century, companies like AT&T, Coca Cola, and Exxon-Mobile, helped create family fortunes, simply because investors owned shares of these household brands. Behind the scenes, these companies were more than just household brands; they were multi-national corporations earning millions, and because of that their stock prices rose dramatically. There are similar investment opportunities that exist for you today with technology and social media stocks.

Prior to the 21st century, the US stock market had been the financial playground of the world's wealthy people. In easy to understand layman's terms, the US Stock Market had been a place where the rich could easily grow their wealth through superior stock selection. Before the 21st Century if you were connected to the right broker, who understood investments trends, IPO's, and corporate earnings, he or she could make you a small fortune because of their financial education.

However, the Worldwide Web changed all of that. With the advent of the Internet, the average investor now has unprecedented access to free research, charting and analysis, and statistics.

Nonetheless, access to information means nothing without a

financial education. The same opportunity that exists for billionaires exists for you in today's stock market. Although you may start with less capital, if you choose the right stocks and follow a proven strategy, you can create financial freedom sooner and faster than you could never imagine.

The stock market has changed my life and enabled me to enjoy and participate in the world in ways I could only imagine. If I can do it, so can you.

Today I spend a portion of my life educating investors on how easy it is to create financial freedom and long-term wealth for themselves and their family.

In this book I will educate you on how the stock market functions so that you can move past fear and participate in the greatest wealth-building vehicle in the world. You have a lot to look forward to.

To help you, I've included easy-to-follow charts and simple analysis.

We will start with looking at how and why a company goes public, and how anyone with an online brokerage account can play the financial investment game alongside today's millionaires and billionaires.

What is an IPO?

No one denies the sexy allure of stock offered by a company's initial public offering (IPO). Visions of capitol gain and future profits cloud the mind during a mad rush to buy, buy, and buy!

Let us explore the process of an IPO, that is, when a privately owned company goes public. What's the difference? Who wins? Does anybody lose? What about the law? Can I buy some shares? Can anybody? What roll does the SEC play? And finally, perhaps the only question that really matters: Should I invest?

An initial public offering, or IPO, is the first sale of stock by a company to the public. A company can raise money by issuing either debt or equity. If the company has never issued equity (sold shares/stock) it's known as an IPO.

Typically companies fall into two broad categories: private and public. A private company is just that: private. Owned by one or more individuals who are accountable only to themselves and as the law requires. A private company might have shareholders but the *amount* of shares is many thousands less than that of a public company or corporation. Private companies also enjoy less scrutiny and oversight than their public counterparts: they are not required to disclose financial information to anyone except by law i.e. tax and insurance purposes. You want to know their quarterly sales figures? Good luck. It is generally not possible to buy shares in a private company. You can ask for an investment opportunity but the owners are under no obligation to sell you anything. Conversely, a public company has *already* sold at least a part of itself to the public and shares are traded in the open market of a stock exchange. You don't have to ask anybody anything and may invest as you please. "Going public" indeed...and going public is an entirely different animal than that of a cozy small business.

The Securities and Exchange Commission (SEC) was formed in 1934 by the "Securities Exchange Act" during Franklin D. Roosevelt's presidency and was part of FDR's New Deal. Basically the SEC has federal oversight of the United States' stock and options exchanges. It also enforces securities laws, proposes securities rules, and regulates the securities industry. The Securities and Exchange Commission has vast powers and strict rules. Once a private company starts down the path of an IPO it is immediately subject to SEC scrutiny and required to comply with SEC laws, rules, and regulations including (but not limited to) the formation of a board of directors, quarterly financial reports, shareholder meetings and disclosure of the holdings and transactions held by officers of the company. The SEC is an integral part of the IPO process and one of the first steps to becoming a public corporation is filing a registration statement with this federal watchdog.

So why bother? Why go public? The short answer is cash and a lot of it. The company hopes for more liquidity or cash on hand and can achieve this by selling stocks to the public. The funds may be used in various ways including expansion and re-investment in infrastructure.

Other benefits:

- Offering stock option plans can attract top talent to the company

- Easier to achieve merger and acquisition deals as stock can be used as part of the payment

- Prestige. It is no small task to list a company on a Wall Street stock exchange

It is important to note that there are other -perhaps not benign- motivations for a company to go public. Venture capitalists can fund startups by burning through capitol to generate excitement and then cash-in on the IPO. After that they walk away not having any intention of expanding or developing the company once it goes public. This is referred to as an "exit strategy" and shareholders end up with the short end of the stick. One reason such a plan could succeed is the difficulty of getting good intelligence on startups and IPO companies: there simply isn't much history there. At the end of the day an IPO is just selling stock: investors absolutely need to do their research and due diligence... Buyers beware.

Unless you are on the inside of the deal it is ***very*** difficult to get a piece of a hot IPO. Why? Lets take a look at investment banks and underwriting.

So my new shoe company has taken off and I am completely unafraid of Nike (Wimps!). I decide to go for it and get my company on the New York Stock Exchange. What do I do? I *could* sell shares myself but that really isn't done much (ever) and besides, what do I know about selling stock? I need an investment bank and get on the horn to Morgan Stanley. There are other choices of course, Credit Suisse First Boston or even Goldman Sachs. My thinking is that the big boys know what they are doing and I expect they will tell me if my dreams are even viable. I have heard tales that smaller, less reputable, investment banks will say "yes" to just about anyone who wants to launch an IPO.

In reality investment banks will compete for the opportunity to underwrite an IPO. There is big money to be made after all. How? The owners of the IPO Company *and* the investment bank(s) receive or *buy stocks at a fraction of the price that will be offered to the public.* They get large blocks of stock before that stock is available on the open market. In some cases employees of the IPO Company will also be able to take advantage of this discount and are taken along the IPO ride to receive a huge chunk of cash. Think Microsoft in the 80's.

Once a potential IPO Company has found an investment bank willing to underwrite them they then spend time hammering out details. Details include the amount of money the company hopes to raise, the type of securities to be issued and the distribution of shares prior to the public offering. After agreement is reached on all sides the underwriter pens a registration statement and files it with the Securities and Exchange Commission. This document contains information about the company including financial records, how the capitol raised is to be used, management background, insider holdings and any legal problems. At this point the SEC requires a cooling off period in order to investigate the company and verify that all material information has been disclosed. (It is interesting to note that the SEC is not only a watchdog: the third part of their mission/mandate states: "To facilitate capitol formation"). After the SEC approves the offering a date (the "effective date") is set when the stock will be offered to the public.

During the cooling off period there is a lot of action.

Most underwriters are hesitant to take on all the risk of an initial offering. In order to mitigate the risk they court *other* large institutional investors. The lead underwriter drafts an initial prospectus and takes it on a marketing tour referred to as a "dog and pony show" or, more simply, a "road show." This prospectus contains all the information about the upcoming IPO *except* the effective date and the initial price offered to the public. These two very important bits of info are left blank and highlighted in red, resulting in the expression "Red Herring" in reference to the initial prospectus. The dog and pony show is not targeted to the general public but to *more* investment banks so the lead bank doesn't take all of the risk. A syndicate of investment banks is formed before the IPO is offered to the public. Considerations of the initial issue price offered by the IPO Company (shares) are affected by the size of the syndicate, how much stock has been allocated within the syndicate and, more importantly, market conditions. Not to mention the viability of the company itself.

Where does that leave the individual investor? The only way I have heard of to a get pre-public offering price on an IPO is to already have a ***large*** account with one of the underwriters. And I do mean large. A few thousand dollars really doesn't make much of an impression with Morgan Stanley. The individual investor can buy stock in an IPO of course, but most likely, only *after* the effective date.

Now that you know how IPO's come into existence, as we move forward I will explain to you a bit more about how the stock market functions and how you can change your life financially by becoming an educated wealthy investor.

Apple, Inc. (AAPL)

Photo credit: Yahoo Finance

Did you know that from the year 2000 to 2015, Apple shares (AAPL) increased in value over 100 percent. That means:

$1,000 investment is now worth over $2,000

$10,000 investment is now worth over $20,000

$100,000 investment is now worth over $200,000

$1,000,000 investment is now worth over $2,000,000
Remember, this happened in just a five-year period.

The above example assumes you purchased AAPL shares at $50. Apple is a member of the Dow Jones Industrial Average. This company creates technology products for worldwide distribution.

The Walt Disney Company (DIS)

Photo credit: Yahoo Finance

From the year 2000 to 2015 Disney stock (DIS) prices increased over 200 percent. That means:

$1,000 investment is now worth over $3,700

$10,000 investment is now worth over $37,000

$100,000 investment is now worth over $370,000

$1,000,000 investment is now worth over $3,7000,000

This assumes you purchased DIS share at $30. Disney is a leader in worldwide entertainment and earns billions from its theme parks, TV networks, Motion Pictures and merchandising. In 2013 Disney purchased the rights from Lucas films for the Star Wars movie franchise, for $3.2 billion dollars.

With both of these stocks, one million dollars invested would have turned into millions. Because of the stock market the rich get richer and with the right financial education so can you.

Questions:

How many shares of this these companies do you own right now?

Have you been programed for financial success?

Do you expect money to work for you?

Do you expect great things to happen for you financially?

What are you focused on right now?

Chapter One:
Success is a Series of Positive Habits

Turns out the old saying is true, success does leave clues. You can change your financial life within ninety days if you're willing to change a few of your negative habits. This book will show you what you need to change in order to increase your wealth in five years or less.

For this book our definition of the rich refers to those individuals who have a net worth of one million dollars or more. These days you can achieve financial freedom sooner than you think. One million dollars is not what it used to be.

The rich develop and pass down positive habits. Some of these habits are directly connected to money, like following a financial plan, but others are not. Because of their positive habits the rich intentionally program their children for financial success. Perhaps what is most surprising is what the wealthy teach their children about money, and it's important role in life.

While doing research for this book I quickly learned one thing; most wealth is hidden. It can't easily be seen by the naked eye. There are many millionaires who still work for a living because their money is locked up in a 401K or investment property they purchased seven years ago. These folks would only have access to their millions if they liquidated everything. In other words, they are rich on paper. However, positive habits got them to seven figures.

You may look at today's millionaires with wonder or amazement. You may ask yourself, how did they achieve it? The next few chapters will show you how.

Even if you think you're late to the party, there's still time for you to achieve financial freedom. First you need to get acquainted with the three types of wealth:

Self-Made Wealth

Very often self-made wealth is created from small businesses that grow exponentially in a short period of time. That short period of time is typically ten years. Businesses that grow within a ten-year period of time can often be sold for seven figures or more.

Examples of businesses that grow exponentially are doctor offices, dentist offices, law firms, dry cleaners and nursing homes. These businesses allow an entrepreneur to create a brand, build that brand, and cash out big by selling that brand in an up economy.

Selling a business also allows the business owner to cash out or stay on as a paid employee. Those who choose to stay on and work for a few bucks will typically take a salary, a consulting fee, and/or participate in a percentage of gross revenue.

Married Wealth

In this day and age there are people who still marry for money. It's a secretive tradition that will never disappear. However, married wealth often comes with strings attached.

Inherited wealth

Inherited wealth happens when loved ones leave seven figures in real estate and life insurance policies.

When you think about Sir. Richard Branson, you're probably picturing hot-air balloons, extravagant cruises, fast cars and beautiful women. Most people perceive the lifestyles of the mega-rich as being full of lavish spending, opulence and grand gestures. The truth is somewhat different.

In reality, tremendously successful people often find pleasure in surprisingly normal and mundane activities. This is important to know, because if you're ever going to be financially successful, you can't have misconceptions about what being rich and famous entails. Here are some things highly successful people like doing that you might not know about:

1. They like helping other people.

Most people think of CEOs and business owners as money-grubbing, cutthroat individuals who only care about themselves. That plays well in TV shows and motion pictures. You might be surprised to learn that successful business owners spend a lot of their time and money giving back to the community.

2. They like the comfort of their own home.

Having a lot of money means that, if you choose to do so, you could stay in the most luxurious hotels all over the world. But most successful CEOs travel so much, they actually look forward to sleeping in their own beds. There truly is no place like home.

3. The super rich have normal hobbies.

Successful business owners like to indulge themselves in simple things. Some like to play a musical instrument while others take up gardening or painting.

4. They love hard work.

If you've got millions of dollars in the bank, you wouldn't work a day in your life, right? Wrong. Wealthy people are addicted to the rewards of hard work. They don't find a lazy, stress-free existence desirable.

The really rich do in fact work. They just work at things that earn millions.

5. The rich cherish their solitude.

One of the by-products of success is being thrust into the limelight. Since they're already such public figures, most of the really rich enjoy spending quiet moments by themselves or with their loved ones whenever possible.

Chapter Two: The Organized Millionaire

Most self-made millionaires are very organized. They have an inherent need to keep their lives in order. Order, structure, and lack of clutter allow self-made millionaires to stay focused.

If your desire is greater financial freedom, you must reduce clutter.

Reduce the Clutter in Your Life to Be More Productive

When you use an app, a game or a website, you're dealing with a user interface. If the interface is designed well, you're able to use the tool to accomplish your tasks efficiently. Your life, or the way you interact with the world, can also be thought of as a user interface. And if your interface is faulty or confusing, your life can be riddled with anxiety, frustration and depression.

Here are some ways in which you can redesign the interface of your life and make it more effective:

1. Eliminate productivity-stealing notifications.

You're at your desk, engrossed in thought, hard at work on an important task. Out of nowhere, the bottom right of your screen flashes with a warning. It's your email server reminding you that you've got new mail. Then, your phone buzzes and you see that you've received a direct message on Twitter. Instantaneously, your train of thought has been derailed by the notifications that you surround yourself with.

When you're working, try to keep your pop-up notifications to a minimum. Put your phone on silent mode. Disable push notifications for your RSS feeds, social media applications and instant messengers. If someone really wants to get in touch with you, they'll call. You can check Twitter once you're done with work.

2. Simplify your goals and habits.

Suppose you've decided to go to the gym after work three times a week. What are the things that need to happen before you even step onto the treadmill? First, you have to put your workout clothes and water into your gym bag. Then, you have to drive to the gym, get a parking spot, change, and find an empty machine so you can begin exercising. After a long day at work, you may be setting yourself up for failure. How much motivation do you think you'll have to do all of these activities when you return home after a hectic day of work?

Instead, try to stack the odds in your favor. If you've been leading a completely sedentary lifestyle, instead of making the commitment to join a gym, consider adopting a bodyweight workout program instead. This way, you don't have to leave your home or find any extra equipment. An empty spot on the floor is all you need to do some push-ups and squats. Use this logic to simplify other goals in your life that are being neglected because they're too complicated to pursue.

3. Use ad-blockers.

Every Internet user can relate to the experience of Googling some information, only to be bombarded with seventeen different ads and pop-up videos before the website even loads. Aggressive advertisements are annoying and take away from the experience of consuming the information you need.

To avoid this problem, try to use ad-free services whenever you can. Install *Ghostery* or *Adblock* on your preferred browser. Use services like *Clearly by Evernote*, which strips the non-textual part of the page and allows you to read articles without being inundated by ads. Look at your inbox and unsubscribe from all of the newsletters that don't serve your needs.

4. Keep your important goals front and center.

Ineffective user interfaces that keep important information hidden from view are frustrating to use. The same is true in life.

The momentum of your daily life can make it hard to keep the big picture in mind. You'll end up working aimlessly, keeping yourself busy for the sake of being busy, and not knowing why you're doing it in the first place.

If you're losing sight of your goals, the best thing to do is keep them in a place where they will be impossible to miss. For example, if your goal is to lose 10 pounds in the next three months, write it down on a piece of paper and stick it to your monitor, your bathroom mirror and below the keyboard on your laptop. This way, you'll be looking at your goal several times a day and this realization will guide your choices. If you find you're wasting too much time on Facebook or 9GAG, use an extension that blocks these websites after you've been on them for a certain amount of time. Put the books you want to read right next to your computer monitor. Go to the startup settings on your browser and make it so that every time you fire up the application, it loads up the draft section on your blog.

The way you interact with the world can be tweaked and customized to create a user experience that is productive, satisfying, and effective for your life. Take the time to think about all of the things that are stealing your attention away from the important things in your life. Once you consciously start removing all of the clutter, you'll experience life differently.

No matter the size of your bank account, you can model your financial habits on those of the wealthy. Many people assume that millionaires must be free spenders, but for the most part that is not the case. For every rap star or basketball player throwing lavish parties and wasting money foolishly, there are a hundred ordinary millionaires watching their budgets and thinking about the long-term consequences of all the money they spend.

Make a Budget and Stick to It

One of the things most millionaires have in common is the ability to manage their money wisely. It just stands to reason that those who have been able to accumulate a million dollars in assets have learned how to live on less than they earn. Without that basic ability, no amount of income would be sustainable.

Simply put, millionaires are good at creating realistic budgets for their household, and even better at sticking to those spending limits. You can learn from their experience by creating your own household budget and tracking all your expenses.

It may take some time to get your budget right, but once you do you will be able to see where every dollar is coming from - and where it is going. That ongoing analysis makes it easier to identify opportunities to cut back and find money to invest.

Control Investment Expenses

The ability to control investment expenses is another thing most millionaires have in common. Investment expenses can really eat into your returns, especially over the long term. Since millionaire investors are particularly good at focusing on the long term, they naturally look at the impact of those ongoing expenses.

Wealthy investors also tend to be comfortable making their own investment decisions. They often use discount brokers to buy and sell stocks, saving themselves a lot of money in the process. If you are not ready to invest on your own, paying for an hour or two with a fee-only investment advisor can be a great way to build your portfolio and reduce your risk.

Track Your Accounts but Don't Obsess Over Them

Pay attention to your money. This is big.

Tracking investment returns is important, and something that millionaires tend to do quite well. Wealthy investors understand the importance of monitoring their investments and rebalancing their portfolios as needed.

Millionaire investors also understand the difference between monitoring their investments and obsessing over them. They know that the market does not always go up, and they resist the urge to panic when things are bad. Wealthy investors were able to weather the recent financial storm due in part to their discipline and their ability to focus on their long-term goals.

Set Short-Term and Long-Term Financial Goals

One thing wealthy investors have learned to do is set both short-term and long-term financial goals. Knowing the difference between the two makes choosing investments easier and helps investors maintain the discipline that is so important to successful money management.

You can follow their examples by setting attainable short-term goals - like getting out of debt or building an emergency fund. As those parts of your financial life come together, you can start setting long-term goals - like boosting your retirement account or saving for a child's education.

Prioritize Your Savings

Making saving and investing a priority is another common trait of millionaire investors. Those wealthy investors have learned to put their savings first, treating their investment account deposits as just another monthly expense.

You have many ways to follow that valuable example. You can automate your savings simply by signing up for your employer's 401(k) or 403(b) plan. Since the money comes straight out of your paycheck, you do not even have to think about it.

You can also put your savings on automatic by setting up monthly transfers from your bank account to your mutual fund or brokerage account. By treating your investments as just another monthly expense, you learn to live on less than you make while giving your portfolio a kick-start.

Prioritize Your Spending

One of the reasons millionaires are able to automate their savings is because they are so good at prioritizing their spending. Wealthy investors have the same kinds of bills as the rest of us, from monthly mortgage payments to health insurance and childcare expenses. What sets them apart is their ability to prioritize their spending and determine which expenses are essential and which are not.

Those wealthy investors are also better than most at distinguishing wants from needs. You might think that the premium cable package or top-shelf cell phone plan is a necessity, but a wealthy investor might look at those things as unnecessary expenses. The ability to prioritize spending and make the most of every dollar is one more thing that separates wealthy investors from the rest of us.

It is tempting to think that every millionaire was born with a silver spoon in his or her mouth, but that is simply not the case. The vast majority of millionaires are self-made. Understanding what they are doing right and emulating it, is the best way to secure your own financial future.

Time Warner Cable Inc. (TWC)

Photo credit: Yahoo Finance

From the year 2000 to 2015 Time Warner Cable Inc. shares (TWC) increased in value over 200 percent. That means:

$1,000 investment is now worth over $3166

$10,000 investment is now worth over $31,660

$100,000 investment is now worth over $310,660

$1,000,000 investment is now worth over $3,166,000

The above example assumes you purchased Time Warner Cable shares at $60. Time Warner Cable is a major provider of cable services throughout the United States.

The Home Depot, Inc. (HD)

Photo credit: Yahoo Finance

From the year 2000 to 2015 Home Depot shares (HD) increased in value over 200 percent. That means:

$1,000 investment is now worth over $3,444

$10,000 investment is now worth over $34,400

$100,000 investment is now worth over $344,000

$1,000,000 investment is now worth over $3,440,000

The above example assumes you purchased Home Depot shares at $35. Home Depot is a major provider of home improvement and construction products and services throughout the United States.

NetFlix, Inc. (NFLX)

Photo credit: Yahoo Finance

From the year 2000 to 2015 Netflix shares (NFLX) increased in value over 800 percent. That means:

$1,000 investment is now worth over $9,000

$10,000 investment is now worth over $90,000

$100,000 investment is now worth over $900,000

$1,000,000 investment is now worth over $9 million

The above example assumes you purchased Netflix shares at $10. Netflix is the largest Internet television network delivering film and TV content via the Internet.

One again this increase happened in just a five-year period.

Again I ask you:

How many shares of these companies do you own right now?

Have you been programed for financial success?

Do you expect money to work for you?

Do you expect great things to happen for you financially?

What are you focused on most?

Chapter Three:
Get to Know the Stock Market;
The Fast Lane to Financial Success

There are many ways to get rich and create wealth in your life. Some choose multilevel marketing while others choose real estate investments. However, the world's wealthiest individuals choose the stock market.

What are the benefits of owning, investing, and trading stocks? When you own stocks, you literally own a portion of a company. Your slice of the pie is called a share. Good companies see their share price rise when the company earns profits (revenue). Why is it more people seek to invest in stocks? It starts with how they are educated.

Money management and saving and investing strategies are not topics that are covered in a high school or general college curriculum. Yet, as adults this education is a necessity. Learning how to invest will make a profound difference in every aspect of your life, as your wealth governs where you live, how you raise your children, and how you retire. Now, more than ever, Americans need to be financially educated.

Over the past fifty years, trading stocks has been perceived as a game only the rich can play. However, the Internet and technology have changed the landscape for the small investor. Today there's greater access than ever to free online stock research, and online brokerage houses like E-trade, have made buying and selling stocks online easy. These developments represent the removal of two key barriers for an individual investor to enter the stock market and manage their own money. There is no reason why anyone can't participate in building wealth through online investing.

Tips for Getting Started

1. **Start Early.**
   Putting money away in an investment account works best if you start early. Your thirties can be a great time to start investing. Money grows best when it has time to mature.

2. **Start Small.**
   Begin by investing with small amounts of money. Even fifty or a hundred dollars per month can add up over a three-year period.

3. **Invest Regularly.**
   Wealth is nothing more than a series of positive financial habits. Most self-made millionaires are in the habit of investing money on a regular basis and at regular intervals.

4. **Set Goals for Your Money.**
   Setting goals is very important. When you set goals, you're actively designing your financial future. When you view the future as a canvas in financial terms, you can paint whatever you want.

5. **Learn How to Invest and Trade Stocks.**
   When you own stocks in publically traded companies, you own a portion of the company. In the stock market any investor can own shares in well-known companies like McDonalds, Coca Cola and Verizon. These companies are part of the Dow Jones Industrial and produce billions of dollars in profit every quarter. As a result, their stock prices tend to rise. Best of all, their shares trade for less than one hundred dollars. An investor can start with nominal shares and watch the value increase over time.

Many investors jump to the conclusion that investment research is useless and that "beating the market" in the long run is not possible. But the long run is precisely when research may achieve its greatest usefulness. It is in the short run that logical evaluation is subject to the foibles of the human mind. For example, analysis can lead one to see patterns where none exist. Our primitive brains are apparently wired to act on impulse by the evaluation of past information – even random data. Investors who rely too much on past information become overly optimistic about stock market winners and overly pessimistic about stock market losers.

This simply means that analysis of past information requires us to examine the long term to make sure that short-term results are validated. Decisions need to be the result of calm analysis of fundamental value.

Investing sometimes involves rigorous work – just like maintaining your home. But investing should not be a constant struggle to follow a lot of rules. Rather, it should be like shopping for bargains at any store…or online. Buying a stock means that you are going to own part of a company. It's that simple. Don't become confused about asset allocation, rebalancing, industry trends, and market sentiment. Just focus on buying companies with promising opportunities for rising profit. What you will actually own is your part of those future profits.

The Significance of P/E Ratios

If you are more of a sophisticated investor, consider this:

If you focus on a company's prospect for future profits, and not periodic fluctuations in the stock price, you are investing not speculating. Spotting a bargain price for the company you are buying is often more art than science. But you can learn this process. You likely already know the most common measure of value. That is, the measurement of how much you are paying for future profits. You pay a price in dollars for each share of stock in the company. Profits are also stated in dollars per share. Hence, the ratio of price per share to earnings per share (the P/E) is a simple measure of value. It's not the only way to measure value, but it's always a good start.

The higher the P/E ratio, the more you are paying for your part of the profit. So, a stock with a big P/E is more "expensive". That doesn't mean the stock in a company with a low P/E is necessarily a bargain, relative to a stock with a higher P/E.

After all, you will own a share of *future* profits, which are unknown guesses. Maybe future profits for a company with a high P/E will rise more than the future profits for a company with a low P/E. In that case, the stock with a high current P/E may be worth owning because the "E" – the earnings – will increase significantly. Similarly, a low P/E stock may have a low "P" – the price – as a reflection of the fact that "E" (earnings) are expected to decrease in the future. But as a general rule, stock in a company with a really high P/E should be avoided; stock in a company with a fairly low P/E is worth considering.

Ready to be even more sophisticated? Take the current P/E ratio – using the present price and the present earnings. Now compare this to the company's average P/E over the last 10 years or even 20 years. That's a reasonably long term. If a company's current P/E is lower than the average, it may be a bargain. That is, the price for the particular company is currently lower *relative to earnings* than has historically been the case. It's like the company is on sale because the cost to own a piece of the company's earnings is lower.

I'm not a huge fan of heavy P/E ratio analysis. If you take P/E ratios too literally you would have ignored stocks like Netflix (NFLX) and Tesla (TSLA), both of which have doubled in price over the last 5 years.

Now you're on you way to learning some simple approaches for examining individual stocks.

The Right Financial Education Is Key

When you trade stocks, your income potential is unlimited. Many of my students in The Wealthy Investor program earn anywhere from $5,000 to $10,000 per month.

Following The Wealthy Investor rules and guidelines can help you consistently build wealth.

Here are three important principles for wealthy investing:

1. **We Don't Marry Stocks, We Only Date Them**
   In the 21st century, our world is changing at a very fast pace. The company that is the dominant player in a sector today can be a laggard tomorrow. Therefore, we only date/invest in a company that is making money (growing revenue) and maintaining leadership in it's sector of the marketplace.

2. **Invest In Companies That Grow Revenue**
   Stock prices rise based on the company's quarterly and annual revenue. Don't buy the stock if you don't understand the story. In other words, as an investor if you don't understand how a company earns money, you don't know the story.

3. **Look Toward the Future**
   Will the company you are investing in be relevant in the next five years? No one can predict the future, but by keeping this question in mind you will be one step ahead of the uneducated self-directed investor.

These three principles keep you focused on strong revenue producing companies and future profits.

Visa Inc. (V)

Photo Credit: Yahoo Finance

From the year 2000 to 2015 Visa's stock price increased over 300 percent. That means:

$1,000 investment is now worth over $3,200

$10,000 investment is now worth over $32,000

$100,000 investment is now worth over $320,000

$1,000,000 investment is now worth over $3,200,000.

NIKE, Inc. (NKE)

Photo Credit: Yahoo Finance

That means:

$100,000 invested is now worth over $200,000

$1,000,000 in now worth over $2,000,000

In my Wealthy Investment Program I teach my students to take out their initial investment and allow their profits to appreciate in value.

Chapter Four:
Be Like Warren Buffet

As of November 2015, Warren Buffet's net worth is estimated at $53.5 billion dollars. Mr. Buffet is known for taking a long-term view of the stock market and investing.

You don't have to be a billionaire to trade and invest like the rich. The Warren Buffet approach to stock market investing works. Mr. Buffet owns 400 million shares of Coca Cola. How did he acquire those shares? The answer is: over time.

Typically, the rich compose portfolios of real estate, bonds and stocks. They build these portfolios over time. What makes Warren Buffet different is instead of buying shares in a given company, he purchases the whole company and becomes the largest shareholder.

This is clearly not a strategy that many can afford to employ, but investing in the stocks that comprise the Dow Jones Industrial is what large institutions do everyday. Any investor can create long-term wealth by purchasing shares of Dow components and buying more once the stock rises.

If you're not Warren Buffet but would like to enhance your wealth over time, it makes sense to own shares of Dow stocks and purchase more every few months.

Create a financial plan that will help you add money to your self-directed brokerage account. Even $250 a month added to an online trading account is a major step. Success is a series of positive habits and any investor can create a plan for the long term just like the rich.

The online stock brokerage industry is more competitive than ever. Almost all online brokers charge less than $10.00 per trade. For the average investor who makes only a handful of trades per month the difference between a $3.00 per trade commission and an $8.00 per trade commission is insignificant. Instead of choosing a broker solely based on the cost per trade you should weigh several other factors before signing up with an online broker.

Level of Service

When researching online brokers you should ask yourself how much help you will need from your broker. Deep discount brokers offer the lowest commissions but they offer very little, if any, advice and support. These brokers are great if you have a lot of investing experience and want to trade on your own.

Other online brokerage firms offer telephone and online support with registered stockbrokers. These stockbrokers will answer your simple investing questions and give you limited advice. This can be perfect if you have some investing experience but feel that you still need a limited amount of guidance.

On the other hand, there are some online brokerage firms that provide a high level of service and advice. You can speak with stockbrokers on the phone or meet with a broker in a regional office. They can assist in trade execution as well as retirement planning and asset allocation. If you need expert advice or help with financial planning, a firm that offers in-person consultations is probably the best choice for you.

Access to Research and Investing Tools

Before choosing a broker, you must also decide if you need research reports and online investing tools. Many online brokers offer Wall Street research reports to their clients. If this is important to you, find out if the broker has adequate access to research reports for the stocks that you invest in. Also, some discount brokerages charge extra for research reports, which should be taken into consideration when calculating the total expenses of working with the broker.

If you need access to online investing tools such as stock screening or back testing software be sure that the software is available from the broker and that it meets your needs. Some brokers offer very basic investing tools while others have very powerful and robust tools. In most circumstances an online broker will allow you to take a trial of their investing tools before you become a client. Also, be sure to find out if there are any costs associated with using the investing tools.

Ability to Meet All of Your Investing Needs

Finally, be sure that the online brokerage can handle the types of investments that you plan on trading. Most online brokers offer their clients the ability to trade domestic stocks, bonds, mutual funds and ETFs. If you plan on trading other types of investments or derivatives such as options, futures, commodities or stocks listed on foreign exchanges, you will need to research whether the brokerage firm can accommodate your needs. Also, if you plan on trading on margin you should ask about the brokerage's rules for margin accounts and the interest rate that they charge for margin interest.

Although most investors look solely at the commissions that online brokers charge, it is vital to dig deeper when choosing a broker. As an investor you have specific needs based on your investing experience, amount of service desired, and the tools and research that you require. Analyzing the offerings of several online brokers will help you find the online broker that is the perfect fit for you.

Costco Wholesale Corporation (COST)

From the year 2001 to 2016 Costco stock (COST) was on fire and increased more than 100 percent. That means:

$1,000 invested become over $2,250

$10,000 invested became over $22,250

100,000 invested become over $222,250

1Million invested became over $2.2 Million

At anytime you could sell your shares, take profits and purchase a new home.

Amazon.com, Inc. (AMZN)

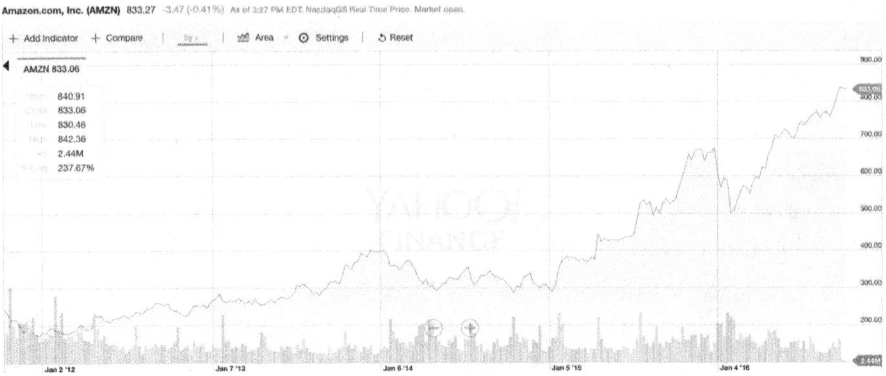

From the year 2001 to 2016 Amazon.com stock (AMZN) hit new highs and increased more than 300 percent. That means:

$1,000 invested become over $4,000

$10,000 invested became over $40,000

100,000 invested become over $400,000

1Million invested become over 4 Million

The rich get rich investing in the stock market.

At anytime you could sell your shares, take profits and pay for your kids college tuition.

Chapter Five:
What The Rich Tell Their Kids

What do you teach your children about money? Whatever it is you teach them will affect their financial future. You can't pass on an education you don't have. If you don't have a financial education, you are increasing the odds that your child will financially struggle.

The cost of buying a home, feeding a family, and sending a child to college, will rise consistently over the next ten years. The truth is your children will need more money than you in the future.

The rich teach their kids the importance of money. They take their kids to work often. They attend charity events. Over dinner they explain how businesses fail and succeed. They also talk about stock investments and ownership. These actions and discussions program their children for success.

If you want your son or daughter to enjoy a happy and healthy financial life, fostering a lifelong love of investing can be a smart move. Kids who grow up in money-smart households are more likely to invest their own money wisely when they enter the workforce. Those smart investing decisions can provide many benefits, from a chance at early retirement to fat college funds for their own children.

One of the best ways to create that lifelong love of investing is to choose investments your kids will love. There are many kid-friendly stocks out there, from video game manufacturers to fast food joints and entertainment companies. Making your son or daughter a part owner of these great companies, is a terrific way to take the mystery out of investing and make it something exciting.

There are several ways to make your kids part owners in the companies they love. You can buy framed stock certificates for a number of kid-friendly companies - from Disney to McDonalds - and give them as gifts. Those beautifully framed stock certificates make wonderful gifts, and they can become treasured family heirlooms.

Older kids may prefer to invest in their favorite companies directly. If you have a brokerage account already, you can set up a minor account for your child and invest that way. If the account is with a discount broker, the cost of investing can be quite low. There are also direct investment programs like *ShareBuilder* that allow you to buy shares directly from the companies. Those programs can be quite inexpensive, especially if you invest on an ongoing basis.

No matter how you choose to invest, here are some kid-friendly companies to consider. Chances are these companies are already involved in your child's life, so investing in them allows your son or daughter to share in the success.

1. **Walt Disney** - even if your child has never been to a Walt Disney World resort, he or she is familiar with the company. From movies and games to TV shows and branded merchandise, the Disney name is everywhere.

2. **Hasbro** - Hasbro is a big name in toys, and it can be a good choice for your child's investment portfolio as well. You can expect your son or daughter to look at brand names a bit more closely after becoming part owner of the Hasbro Corporation.

3. **McDonalds** - the golden arches are one of the first things kids learn to recognize, and chances are your own kids have been there a time or two. Your child can enjoy the stock they own every time they enjoy a Happy Meal.

4. **Coca Cola and Pepsi** - soft drinks are big business, and many kids learn to love these brands early. Even if your son or daughter is not allowed to drink soda, they can share in the future of these ubiquitous brands.

5. **Foot Locker** - chances are your kids have already chosen their favorite brands of sneakers, and Foot Locker sells

most of them. Becoming part owner of this company is a great way to profit from the popularity of those new sneaker styles.

6. **Electronic Arts** - if your kids love video games, they have probably enjoyed an Electronic Arts release. Give them the gift of Electronic Arts shares and let them share in the fun.

7. **Microsoft** - Microsoft makes some of the most successful gaming consoles in the world, as well as the operating systems that power their favorite devices. Becoming part owner in this company is a great way to get your kids excited about investing.

Chances are these companies are already involved in your child's life, so investing in them will allow your son or daughter to share in the success.

Many people who should be happy do not allow themselves that privilege. The average life span worldwide is about 70 years, and U.S. citizens can expect to live for about 80 years, so there should be enough time to be happy. Yet, according to a recent survey, the average American can expect to spend about a quarter of their life being unhappy.

One reason for this dissatisfaction with life is that most people do not take the time to differentiate between their needs and their wants. Needs provide people with basic comfort and safety, whereas wants are not necessary to survival.

For example, someone living in a small apartment with decent furniture, food to eat and adequate employment has everything they need, so they should be happy. But if this same person decides they need to own a house, but finds they cannot afford one, failure to accept this need as a want can cause that person to feel depressed and lose what happiness they had.

The problem of turning a want into a need also exists on a smaller scale. It could relate to buying a new car, a smartphone or even something as simple as the latest album by a popular artist. "Keeping up with the Joneses" is a sad game that encourages people to sacrifice their happiness in exchange for a lifestyle that is not their own.

There is no reason for you to forget your dreams of a better life, but you should not waste the happiness you experience today. Making your dreams come true is usually possible with hard work and a plan, but you should remember to take care of your present reality and happiness.

Realizing and maintaining happiness is much simpler if you learn to recognize the difference between desire and necessity.

Gratitude Forces Abundance to Multiply

In this book I've exposed several habits of the rich and super rich. Choose the ones that work for you and your life will change. More than anything money, wealth and financial abundance create freedom of choice. Gratitude will jump-start the process.

At this moment, you are blessed! You have a lot to be grateful for. Look at what you already have and learn to see the value in it. If you are already reasonably happy, work to retain that happiness while planning a financial future where your dreams are fulfilled and you are even better off

Chapter Six:
The Power Of Focus and Your Money

You have the power to be rich.

You have the power to shape your financial future.

Your thoughts and money beliefs are very powerful.

Creating wealth is all about focus!

The Law of Attraction tells us in this life you get more of what you focus on. If you focus on negativity and lack, more often then not you will find yourself with less money and less happiness. By contrast, if you focus on creating wealth you can have financial freedom sooner rather than later.

Focus is a learned behavior. As children we learn from our family and primary care givers many things, including the importance of money. Depending on your background, you either learned that money is hard to come by or that money should work for you as a tool to make your life easier.

I grew up being told that life would be difficult and money would be hard to come by. I was born into a lower socio-economic working class family and raised by a single mother. Everyone around me worked for a living. Everyone around me struggled financially. That's just the way it was.

One of the most popular phrases in my house was "money don't grow on trees." I took that to mean that I was lucky if I would be able just to pay my bills each month with little left over. This created in me negative thoughts around money and financial success.

Today I have more wealth than anyone in my family. This happened because I learned to change my negative thoughts about money and to enhance my ability to earn large amounts of it. I learned to expect good things to happen for me financially. I also taught myself how to change my focus.

Along my journey I started to study the rich. I learned that if I truly desired to have financial freedom, I needed to study how wealthy people think and what they teach their children.

It turns out the rich and the super rich teach their children that money and people should work for them. They teach them that they should expect money to produce positive results and support their lifestyle. Therefore, the children of the rich expect great things to happen for them financially. They expect money to multiply. They expect the stock market to help them generate millions and even billions of dollars per year.

I share my story with you, so that you can see the link between your thinking and your financial success. Your thoughts are very powerful.

As a success teacher, speaker, stock market trader and recognized author, I aim to help others. It's how I add a powerful dose of positivity to the world. If I help you earn money trading and investing in the stock market within the next sixty days, I only ask one thing in return. It's that you take a small portion of your profits and help someone. That includes giving a few dollars to your favorite charity or religious organization. Together we can make a positive contribution to our world.

Time To Focus on Stocks

In today's world it's difficult to log onto the Internet and avoid stories about the accomplishments of billionaires like Bill Gates who started Microsoft, or billionaire Mark Zuckerberg, founder of Facebook. Their innovations are changing how we buy products and communicate.

Today Bill Gates has an estimated net worth of fifty-four billion. Mark Zuckerberg has an estimated net worth of thirty-eight billion. Although not widely publicized in the media, both of these gentlemen have made shareholders rich. Because of technology you and I can easily go along for the ride. We have easy access to the greatest wealth creation tool in the world...The Stock Market.

Before we go on, there is one point I'd like to clarify. This book is not about financial greed. Instead it's about raising your consciousness and changing your focus so that even if you know nothing about investing you can participate and benefit from the revolution that is changing the planet this every minute.

Wall Street is financing innovation like never before. As an investor you can ride along.

Part of being a successful investor is learning to change your attitude towards money and seeing it as an unlimited tool rather than a finite resource. Let's explore the difference between the two approaches.

Seeing Money as a Resource

Many of us think of money purely as a resource, something that comes and goes throughout our lives. This perspective means that we tend to focus on the scarcity, or lack of money. We're always concerned about where money is coming from, fearful about how much we're spending and always wishing that we could earn more. Money becomes an obstacle to achieving what we want in life.

Seeing Money as a Tool

A healthier way to approach money is to see it as a tool. This change of attitude means that we think about its potential, rather than its scarcity. When we understand that money is a tool and resource that we have the power to use, it can transform our attitude towards our finances. We understand that with careful decisions, patience and common sense; we can use our wealth to generate more money and achieve our financial and life goals.

Thinking Like a Millionaire

Seeing money as a tool and a resource is what millionaires do. They take the money they already have and use it to invest over the medium to long-term, with the belief that they will grow their wealth through patience and diversification.

Seeing money as a tool instead of a resource means that we understand money's potential. Although we know that our finances are in a constant state of change, we're able to approach them objectively and take the emotion out of them. This is a more relaxed way of understanding wealth and is a useful starting point for being a successful investor.

What You Can Do

If you want to be successful investor, a good place to start is to examine how you see money and understand what you can do to change your thinking. What is your attitude towards money right now? Do you see it as a resource or do you see it as a tool? If you see your finances purely as a resource, what can you do to change your attitude?

Try to think about your money in a more objective way; see your disposable income as something that you can directly use to grow your wealth.

It may be impossible to stop worrying about money altogether, but developing an objective, dispassionate approach will reduce the stress that you feel. Changing your attitude towards money takes time. It isn't an instantaneous shift.

Your perspective will change gradually, and as it does, you'll start to see that money can have a positive and helpful influence on your life. You can use that attitude, together with the power of patience and time, to help you grow your wealth.

Twitter, Inc. (TWTR)

Not every technology company that goes public produces stellar results for investors.

From January 2014 to 2016 Twitter (TWTR) disappointed investors as it failed at generating revenue.

Although Twitter is a great platform for communications, the company fails to be able to generate advertising dollars.

$1,000 invested in TWTR in 2014 by 2016 worth $278

$10,000 invested in TWTR in 2014 is was worth $2,780

$100,000 invested in TWTR was worth $27,800

No one on Wall Street like owning a losing stock.

The Clorox Company (CLX)

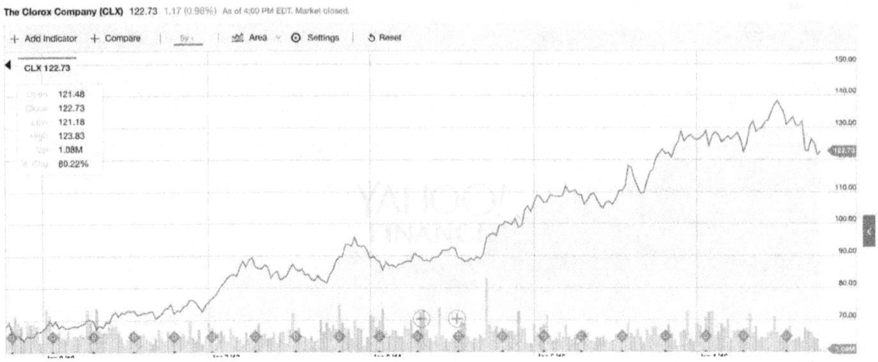

By contrast, The Clorox Company (CLX), whose brands include Formula 409, Liquid-Plumr, Pine-Sol, S.O.S, and Tilex, did very well for investors.

From 2012 to 2016 CLX performed very well.

$1,000 invested 2012 became worth $1,890

$10,000 became worth over $18,900

$100,000 became worth over $189,000

$1 million became worth over $1.8 million

Want to be a successful stock market investor?
Focus on learning how to choose good long-term investments.

Chapter Seven:
Want to Become a Millionaire? Read This

If you dream of becoming a millionaire, you might think of buying a lottery ticket. While that small investment could indeed turn into a million dollars, the odds against it are quite great. As experts have pointed out, you have a better chance of getting struck by lightening, attacked by a bear or even dating a supermodel than you do of picking the winning numbers for the big drawing.

While there is nothing wrong with buying the occasional lottery ticket and dreaming big, you probably should not rely on the lottery gods to secure your financial future. Fortunately there is a better and surer way to get that million-dollar prize.

If you can spare a mere $10 a day, that small daily investment could grow to over a million dollars in 45 years. That means an 18-year old who just started his first job could retire a millionaire at age 63.

This assumes that the money you set aside grows at an average annual rate of just 7 percent - not an unreasonable figure based on historical stock market performance. If you are able to divert just $10 a day to a low-cost investment like a stock market index mutual fund, you could end up with a million dollars even without that winning lottery ticket.

Putting away $10 a day is not as hard as you might think. If you can do without that morning cup of latte and break the vending machine habit at work, you could easily free up $10 or more. If you are a smoker, giving up that dangerous and unhealthy habit could give you more than enough for your million dollar dreams.

You might even be able to reach your goal by gathering your change every day and throwing those coins in a jar. Imagine becoming a millionaire with just your pocket change.

If you want a fun diversion, go ahead and play the lottery. Just don't count on that little card to fund your retirement dreams. In the long run, you are much better off using that $10 a day to get rich slowly.

The Problem With Mutual Funds

If you already have money in a Mutual Fund, great job! You're off to a great start but there's a problem.

A Mutual Fund is nothing more than a basket of stocks you let someone choose for you. They then charge you a fee for doing so. Mutual funds are a type of investment program for smaller investors. Typically, a Mutual Fund accepts money from thousands of different investors, none of which contribute a majority of the money to the general fund. A manager or team of managers then takes the money from the pool of money contributed by investors, and invests the money into various ventures. Their main objective is to increase the amount of money in the investment pool.

In the eyes of the Securities and Exchange Commission, or the SEC, Mutual Funds are classified as companies. Like any other company, the main objective of a mutual fund is to turn a profit. Investors often choose a mutual fund based on the past performance of the mutual fund's manager. This past performance reflects his ability to choose investments that overall generate a healthy return. Each time you invest in a Mutual Fund you are changed a fee. This fee or "load" can be as much as five percent each time you make a contribution. In the end, fewer of your investment dollars go to work for you.

There's no need to ever be intimidated by the stock market. Owning stocks directly is easy once you have an online brokerage account and an education.

Here the five reasons you should own stocks directly right now:

5) Mutual Funds are nothing more than a basket of stocks you allow some else, a Mutual Fund Manager in most cases, to choose. Why would you trust your retirement to a stranger's taste?

4) When you deposit money into a Mutual Fund, you're often charged a fee called a load. Loads can rage from 2% to 5% percent. Simply stated, you loose 2% to 5% of your funds each time you make a deposit.

3) When you purchase shares of stocks directly though an online trading account like TD Ameritrade, there are no monthly management fees. If the stock that you purchase pays a dividend, the dividend is deposited into your trading account and can be redirected back into stock or spent by you as cash.

2) Stocks increase in value faster than Mutual Funds
For example, Dow Component Disney (ticker DIS) has increased 100% in the last five years. That means a $10,000 investment is now worth over $20,000. You just can't get that kind of performance from a Mutual Fund.

The number one reason to choose stocks over Mutual Funds?

Stocks can bring you consistent monthly income. Yes, owning stocks does require a financial education but that education can pay off big when it comes to earning money monthly.

The Benefits of Online Stock Trading

Why do millionaires invest in stocks? Because investing in the stocks of publicly held companies provides a potential opportunity for investors to earn money and for companies to maintain a positive balance sheet. Online trading, which is the buying and selling of stocks on the Internet, has made it easier for the general public to open an account with a broker, research the best companies in which to invest, and buy and sell stocks. Allow me to expound upon the benefits of online trading for both the investor and the company in which they have purchased shares of stock. I will also outline the beginning steps to online trading.

Putting one's privately held money into a publicly held company that has maintained steady growth will potentially earn money on the money invested. For example, Investor Q has decided to buy $100 of stock in Company X because Company X pays dividends. In other words, Company X will pay a portion of their profit earnings to Investor Q on a regular basis. Depending on the potential of future profits of Company X, Investor Q could possibly earn an income above and beyond his initial purchase of $100 worth of stocks. Investor Q's money is making money.

If Company X does not pay dividends as part of their stock agreement but their stock price rises more often than it falls, Investor Q could possibly hold on to his stock and then sell it for a higher price than at which he bought it thereby increasing the value of his initial investment. The downside of this type of investment is that Company X's stock price may never go any higher than at the time of Investor Q's initial stock purchase. In fact, it may drop in price. Investor Q might end up selling his stock for a lower price and end up losing money.

Company X is offering stock in their company to the general public for mainly one reason: to generate an influx of cash. How they use that cash will determine whether their stock price is going to rise and possibly attract more investors, or fall due to misappropriation of the funds, thereby causing investors to unload the stock from their portfolios. There are several ways Company X can use the cash to increase their bottom line profit. They can use it to pay off lines of credit so all future revenues, after expenses, are profit. Or they can expand their business by allocating the incoming funds towards buying or leasing a bigger building, acquiring more equipment and/or hiring additional employees.

There is always risk of losing money with trading (buying and selling) stocks on the Internet. That is why it is very important for anyone who is considering online trading to do abundant preliminary research in the areas of financial planning, brokers, transaction fees, company performance, economic conditions and investor's fickleness. Stock values can fluctuate from low to high and back down to low again simply because of multiple investor's attitudes. Taking the time to find the best broker for your needs, and the companies with the highest potential for increased profits will minimize, but not completely erase, the risk of financial loss. There are no guarantees of financial gain in the world of online trading but with the right amount of research and financial planning the odds of success increase.

The first step to take before making your initial purchase of stocks is to determine the amount of money you will need to set up an account with a broker, including transaction fees. Does the broker charge an inactivity fee if you only buy stock in one company and hold on to it while making no other trades? Does the broker offer a lower per trade fee if you decide you want to do high volume buying and selling? Having a financial plan and, more importantly, sticking to it will mitigate the chances of overspending. The sole purpose of online trading should be to generate more income for the investor and the company.

Using a reputable online broker can make the online stock trading experience easy and safe. Online brokers store an investor's money and stocks in an account and based on the investor's selections, facilitate the stock trades. An investor should always make sure the online broker's website has high-level security measures to protect against theft and fraud. The website should have an automatic log-out after a certain number of minutes of inactivity on the site and all of the transaction transmissions should be encrypted to discourage hacker attacks.

Online stock trading has opened the floodgates for millions of individuals to buy and sell stocks of brand new start-up companies through IPOs (Initial Public Offerings), and of well-known companies that have been in existence for many years. With adequate financial planning and research, online traders can earn extra income for future events such as college funds and retirement. With incoming cash from offering stock options and no associated interest rates because it is not borrowed money, companies can grow their business, increase their profitability and give a boost to their local economy.

If you want to be a successful investor, learning from the most successful investors is one of the best ways to learn. Skip past the trial and error that bogs down most investors for years (or decades) and adopt the best practices of top investors right now. Here are five habits especially common among smart investors:

1. **Patience.** Intelligent investors are in it for the long haul. It might take many years before a smart investment pays off. In the short term, a good investment can seem stupid - a stock that is still fundamentally strong may tumble. But, the best investors don't try to make a quick buck. Steady, reliable gains over the years are the most reliable way to profit. Take the long view and don't dump a stock just because it is experiencing some temporary troubles.

2. **Commitment.** Strong investors don't sway with the ever-changing wind of opinion. If you try to chase the latest investment trends, you'll constantly be overturning your

investment portfolio. Choosing one or two solid strategies will get you much farther. Don't let the opinions of others have an undue influence on you - good investors have an internal evaluation process that takes precedence over the views of the crowd.

3. **Willingness to fail.** You can't be afraid of failure - because, no matter how good of an investor you are, you will have failures. In fact, many of the best investors have had bigger failures than most; the difference is their triumphs have also been greater. As with the rest of life, investors who are afraid of failure will never take the sort of chances necessary for the biggest success.
In the Wealthy Investor program I teach you how to minimize failure by investing in Dow Stocks first.

4. **Planning.** Setting, and then reaching goals is necessary for investment success. If you don't know what you want from your investment portfolio, you'll make haphazard, semi-random decisions. This is no way to make money. Make concrete plans (i.e., to concentrate your investments in a particular area of the market), and then stick to them. Of course, you can't be too rigid - all strategies need to be periodically reevaluated. Choosing a plan now, though, is the first step.

5. **Resilience.** Strong investors don't let failures hold them back. Reversals should only be speed bumps on your path to success. Possessing the ability to come back from setbacks stronger than ever is crucial. Look at your failures as an opportunity: learn from what you did wrong, and your chances of doing well in the future will increase. The errors in judgment you make in your first years of investing will pave the way for decades of future profits.

Top investors each have their own unique approach. If you join their ranks then you will do so with your own methods and practices. Nonetheless, certain habits are common to almost all of the best investors. Begin your path to becoming a great investor by building up those habits, starting now.

Learning to invest in stocks on your is empowering. Learning how to trade stocks on a part time basis can earn you $500 to $10,000 per month. It's all about having the right financial education.

From this moment on make the commitment to let go of negative programing. Pay attention to what you focus on and your money beliefs. Become a positive force in this world. You can do it! Your children and love ones depend on you.

Focus on stocks and investing because you deserve to be financially free!

Chapter Eight: Earning An Extra $5,560 Per Month

Question. Did you earn $5,560 from the stock market last month?

If you could earn $5,560 per month in part-time hours, what would you do with the extra income? How would your life be different? Most importantly, whom would you help? Keep reading and I'll show you how easy it is to change your life.

First, I have a confession. I love The Stock Market! I love how it has changed my life. For over twenty years I have been trading and investing in the stock market. For over ten years I have been teaching my approach for earning monthly income.

In my Wealthy Investor program I help investors just like you earn $5,000, $10,000, and even $30,000 per month trading stocks from home. Collectively, my Wealthy Investor students and I have earned millions.

Here's the best part of my story. I have never worked for or been employed by a Wall Street firm or Hedge Fund. I'm what's known in the financial arena as a self-directed investor. That means I invest, research and trade stocks without the assistance of a financial professional.

I build wealth in several trading accounts. After twenty years, trading stocks is a natural part of my weekly activities.

To be successful, you don't need to learn complex trading strategies and technical analysis. Complex trades generate commissions for your online brokerage firm. I teach my Wealthy Investor students to keep their stock trading strategies simple. You'll earn a lot of money and pay less in commission as a result of following this rule.

Trading and investing is not gambling, but rather a profession or hobby that can earn you a lot of money. Unlike real estate, there are no credit checks, leaky pipes, window replacements, closing costs, or bank approvals. All you need is an online trading account at a brokerage house like ETrade.com, TDAmerade.com, or Fidelity.com.

In The Wealthy Investor program we track a company's earnings and trends. We produce monthly income by selling covered call options and collecting dividends. In our trading account we set goals and targets. We choose stocks to invest in for the long term, as well as stocks to trade for monthly or weekly income. This is how you earn big profits and invest over the long term.

Here are few things about stocks you should know:

1) The stock market is one game and there are one hundred ways to play it.

2) Stocks can be bought and predictably sold for monthly income.

3) Some stocks carry higher risks than others.

Want to Earn Big Money? Learn to Keep it Simple

The biggest lesson my Wealthy Investor students learn about trading and investing is how to keep things simple. Throughout this e-book I will show you how to earn monthly income from the stock market. All you need is the desire to earn and a willingness to achieve a financial goal.

The Truth About The Stock Market

Make Simplicity your new BFF.

For the last one hundred years the US stock market has been the playground for the wealthy. The top one percent of millionaires create long-term wealth from stocks by investing in stable companies like AT&T, Verizon, Disney and Coca-Cola. Shares of these companies are assets. These assets tend to rise over time. They are also passed down from one generation to the next.

Because of today's high-speed Internet access, hand held devices, and other forms of technology, you have 24/7 access to the game of trading and investing. The playing field has been leveled. Today you can play and win at the investing game.

When it comes to trading stocks you can do well. You can easily learn how to sell covered calls and produce hundreds or thousands of dollars each month. So why don't you already know this? Because your financial adviser will never tell you about income generating strategies for fear that they will lose your business.

Financial advisers earn money off of the fees you pay each month for "managing your money". Once you learn how easy it is to earn monthly income on your own, you won't need a financial adviser. In fact, you'll earn more, reduce your fees, and increase your profits.

Investing in members of the Dow Jones Industrial Average reduces your inherent risk. Companies like IBM, McDonalds, Johnson and Johnson, and JP Morgan have been around for decades and earn billions of dollars worldwide. Shareholders have earned millions over the past ten years alone because the share price of these companies has increased dramatically.

What would you do with a $1,000,000 profit earned in a five-year period for doing nothing but being a shareholder in any one of the above companies?

Let's take it one step further- $10,000,000 is now worth over $20,000,000. Are you starting to get the point? Investing in stocks directly is why the rich get richer.

If you're reading this book, chances are you don't have an extra $10,000,000 just hanging around. I get that. Please don't miss the point. The point is that you still can get rich and make money monthly. Start with a small amount of money and grow it using The Wealthy Investor approach. Now let's dive deeper into the world of trading and investing.

Advanced Degrees Don't Make Millionaires

As I keep emphasizing, if you want to be successful as a stock market participant, learn to keep it simple. As a teacher and trader, the first thing I teach my students is how to keep it simple.

There's no question an advanced degree broadens your world. I'm all in favor of advanced forms of education. However, when it comes to investing you don't need an advanced degree. On Wall Street you don't need a PHD or college credits. The playing field is equal. You are just as smart as your financial adviser. In fact, if you follow my approach to keeping it simple, you'll out-perform most mutual funds and financial advisers.

The moral of the story is that there is a lot of money in simplicity.

Chapter Nine:
Why You Should Be Investing In Stocks

Investing In Stocks

For most investors, the fastest and easiest way to build wealth is to regularly put money into a diversified index tracker or mutual fund and hold that investment for 10 years or more. This reduces risk by using the investing principles of diversification, patience, and "dollar cost averaging."

Although this is the easiest way to invest, it isn't the only way. Many investors also like the idea of holding stocks in individual companies, such as Apple, Disney, Johnson and Johnson, Tesla, or others. However, there are principles to follow if you want to put money into individual stocks.

Be Prepared to Invest for the Long Term

The stock market can be volatile, and individual stocks are even more volatile than the market as a whole. However, the tendency is for the market and most stocks to increase in value over time.

You should be happy investing your money for a minimum of five to 10 years, with longer being better.

If you need to sell stocks sooner than that, there's a chance that you'll lose money. Stock markets tend to run in cycles, and if you sell while the market is in a down cycle (a "bear" market), then it's likely that you'll lose money on your investment. Fortunately, bear markets usually don't last more than a few years, so with patience you'll see your stocks increase in value.

Become Comfortable with Moderate to High-risk Investments

Because stocks are so strongly influenced by the news, economic factors, and worldwide events, they're considered quite risky when compared to other, safer investments such as bonds, trackers, or real estate. As an investor, you'll need to be comfortable with this risk. Although more risk does sometimes mean a higher reward, it can also mean larger losses than you'd see elsewhere. You can reduce your risk by diversifying your investments and holding them for a long period of time.

Learn How to Investigate and Analyze Businesses

A large part of the performance of a stock is based on how well the underlying business is performing. This means it's important to have a good understanding of the company in which you are investing. You'll need to be comfortable with financial reports, investment ratios, and the various other methods that are used to analyze businesses and performance. This is known as "fundamental analysis" and comes in two main forms:

. **Qualitative analysis** -- This involves understanding the context of a business, how it performs compared to its competitors, whether it's a leader in its sector or industry, its projected returns, and various other factors.

. **Quantitative analysis** -- This involves understanding the various financial factors and ratios of a business, including profits, price/earnings, earnings growth, return on assets, and various other ratios.

It does take time to learn and analyze the various factors that can impact a business. There are "stock screening" websites that can help, but you'll still need to understand what they are telling you.

Decide on, and Stick with an Investment Approach

There are many different approaches to identifying and investing in individual stocks. Four of the most common are:

. **Quality stocks** -- Investing in large, blue chip companies that are leaders in their field (e.g., Apple, Shell, AT&T).

. **Income stocks** -- Investing in stocks that pay a good interim return or dividend (e.g., Exon Mobil, General Motors, Verizon).

. **Investing in value stocks** -- Finding unloved, undervalued companies in the hope that they will increase in value (e.g., many utility and industrial businesses).

. **Investing in growth stocks** -- Putting money into businesses that you believe will grow faster than the market as a whole (e.g., Netflix, Tesla, Amazon.com). These three stocks have all been big winners over the past few years and made millions for investors.

You should always buy stocks according to some sort of criteria or strategy. While it's fine to have more than one approach, buying random stocks on a whim isn't a good way to build a solid portfolio.

Take the Time to Reinvest your Dividends

Most stocks pay out interim returns or dividends several times a year, as a reward for holding the stock. These dividends typically range from 1 percent to 4 percent of the overall value of your holding, and when they are paid out, the money will stay in your stock broker account until you decide to do something with it. This means you'll need to review your dividends on a semi-regular basis, perhaps once a quarter, and decide whether to reinvest or withdraw them.

Have a Tax Strategy

When you sell a stock, you'll typically need to pay tax on any profit or capital gain you've made. You should speak to an accountant or tax adviser who can explain how much you owe and how you can reduce your tax in future.

Hold Individual Stocks as Part of a More Diversified Portfolio

Because of market volatility, you should never just hold individual stocks. One of the best ways to reduce your risk is to make various types of investments, at different risk levels and frequencies, for multiple lengths of time.

This type of diversification will help you build a strong, reliable, and resilient portfolio. Ideally, a good portfolio would contain a mixture of individual stocks, trackers, mutual funds, bonds, real estate, and other investment vehicles.

Bringing it all together

Here are the main things to remember when deciding on stock investments:

Volatility and risk -- Investments in individual stocks can be very volatile over the short term; only invest money in individual stocks for the long term, as otherwise you could see a loss. The Wealthy Investor approach lowers risk.

The right approach -- There are different factors that affect your investing approach; review the different approaches so you can understand your potential risks and returns.

Get comfortable with math and analysis -- Look into the fundamental factors, questions, facts, and figures behind a business to make sure that it's something you're comfortable investing in.

Invest to your life goals -- Remember that you should invest so you can meet your life goals. The more you can diversify your investments and the longer you can hold them, the better.

As you can see, investing in individual stocks can take time and effort. Even if you see good returns from individual stocks, they usually do not outperform the market as a whole (since the combined value of all stocks **is** the market as a whole).

Because of this, many investors choose to put money into index trackers, mutual funds, or Exchange Traded Funds (ETFs). These types of investments are typically much easier to manage, are naturally diversified, and track the performance of large parts of the stock market and other areas. Depending on your needs, intent, and the amount of time you have, they might be a good alternative to investing in individual stocks.

Investing to your life goals

The aim of most wealthy investors isn't just to make money. Although part of investing is growing your wealth, it's important to have a strong foundation and know what you're investing towards.

Money is simply a means to an end, and a resource that you use to achieve what you want to in life. If you're serious about investing, you should think about the goals and lifestyle you want, and use that to inform your decisions. Understanding these outcomes will affect the way that you approach investing.

You should spend some time thinking about your goals over the next few years, and how much money you're likely to need. Go through each of your goals and assign them to an immediate, short, medium, or long-term time frame. Next, estimate roughly how much money you're going to need for each one. Once you have a list of life and financial goals, you can then decide on the best investments to help you reach them.

Immediate goals (up to a year)

Your immediate goals are to have enough money to live, on a day-to-day basis. This means having cash to pay the bills, make your mortgage or rent payments, buy groceries, look after yourself, repay your debt, and pay any day-to-day living expenses.

Any money that you need for your immediate future should not be invested. When you know how much you need on a day-to-day basis, keep that amount of money (plus a secure financial buffer) in an account that gives you rapid and easy access.

Short-term goals (one to three years)

Your shorter-term financial goals are what you want to achieve over the next one to three years. This could include going on vacation, buying a car, doing home improvements, or taking part in some other life event. There are not many investments that will give you a guaranteed, healthy return over such a short period of time.

You could choose to put your money into a high interest savings account, a certificate of deposit or some other low-risk investment where you are guaranteed to get a return. The volatility of the stock market makes it a less than ideal place to invest for short-term goals.

Medium-term goals (three to ten years)
These are the life goals that could happen within the next few years. This could include a deposit on a house, saving for a wedding, starting a business, having children, or other major life changes. You should consider three to ten years as the minimum length of time to hold an investment for.

Over this period of time, most investments will increase in value. However, because nothing is guaranteed, you should balance your medium-term financial goals against the level of risk and reward you want to receive from your investments.

Long-term goals (Ten years plus)
These are the financial goals that you want to reach over a longer term. This could include saving for college or your retirement, moving into your dream home, or any other life goal that is on the long-term horizon.

Over this period of time, most investments will increase in value and you can see good returns if you are able to invest for 10 years or more. This is why putting money into a retirement account or other long-term fund is one of the best ways to invest your money.

Naturally your goals are going to change, as you get older. Your financial and life goals in your mid-twenties are going to be very different than when you are in your fifties.

Investing to your life goals is one of the best ways to understand what you want to achieve with your money. Realistically thinking about your life goals and working out roughly how much you're going to need means that you can make strong, practical decisions about how, where, and when to invest. Use these techniques and review your life goals and investments on a regular basis to ensure you're continuing to meet the outcomes that you want. Hitting your investment goals sets the stage for generating trading profits every month.

Now let’s look at one stock strategy that can bring you monthly income.

Chapter Ten:
Covered Calls for Income

Covered calls are Wall Street's hidden strategy. It is my all time favorite strategy because it is repeatable under every market condition. In order to generate large profits you don't need an advanced understanding of technical analysis, you just need the desire to make money and the discipline to keep it simple.

Selling covered calls (aka selling call options or writing covered calls) allows anyone with an online trading account to generate thousands of dollars per month with low risk.

Selling call options on stocks you own is a fast and reliable way of generating income on a monthly basis. As Wealthy Investors we sell covered calls on stocks that are over twenty-five dollars per share. To sell covered calls on stocks you own, you must own a minimum of 100 shares of a given stock. Each 100 share block allows an investor to sell one **contract**.

100 shares = 1 Contract
200 shares = 2 Contracts
1,000 shares = 10 Contracts

Covered Calls work like this:

Let's say you've purchased one hundred shares of XYZ stock at $9.75. That stock is now in your possession. If you wanted to hold that same stock for three years **you are free to do so**. However, if you wanted to generate income from that $9.75 stock you **are free to do so**.

Just moments after you purchased XYZ, you decide you want to sell the stock when it reaches $10. Rather than selling the stock immediately, you could **sell a call option**.

Selling a call option means that you would be selling the right, not the obligation, to someone in the marketplace to buy that stock away from you at the $10 price at a later date. The buyer of the option would then pay you something called a **premium**. In this example, our premium is $.90 per share. The price that you've agreed to sell the stock at is called the **strike price**. In this case it's $10.

Options In Hollywood & The Entertainment Biz

If you are still having trouble understanding options, let's take a look at how options play out in the entertainment business.

Let's say you wrote a film script. You send your script to a well-known Hollywood production company, where the top executive reads it. Although she loves it, she's not one hundred percent certain she can sell your script to a major motion picture studio for production. What's her solution? An option.

The Hollywood production company is willing to option your script from you for $50,000. The option expires in six months. You still own the product and copyright. If a studio picks up your script, you've agreed in advance to sell it to the production company for $250,000.

In the right option scenario, everybody wins.

In the above example, if Warner Bros. selects your script for production, you earn an additional $250,000. However, whether your script gets sold or not, you get to keep the initial $50,000.

Stocks In Strong Upward Trends

XYZ Stock is in a strong upward trend with good earnings. It's currently trading at $14.50 in the month of September.

The next strike price up is $15.

The premium for selling the October $15 call option is $.75 per share.

You own 100 shares of XYZ or 1 contract.

If you sell the October $15 call option for $.75 you will earn $75.

$. 75 x 100 = $75 (or $75 per contract).

The Result of Selling the Option

100 shares at $14.50 produce $75 in premium income

200 shares at $14.50 produce $150 in premium income

300 shares at $14.50 produce $225 in premium income

1,000 shares at $14.50 produce $750 in premium income

If you want to learn even more about covered call writing, visit the **www.WealthyInvestor.net** and download **The Wealthy Investor Guide to Stock Market Success.** In this six CD Audio series I walk you through covered call options in easy to understand language with visual illustrations.

Audio CDs included in **The Wealthy Investor Guide To Stock Market Success** allow you to master the language of this powerful making strategy so that you can begin to profit.

Improve Your Life and Learn How to Invest Your Money

If you often say, "I can't invest money because..." and then give all sorts of reasons why it's not possible, it might be time to start pursuing the opportunities that are available to you. The stock market is a huge opportunity.

Opportunities are possibilities and life is full of possibilities. Simply put, a possibility is something that's possible. It may be something you can do today or it may be something you can investigate today and do at a later date.

Some possibilities are obvious. For example, you might walk past a window and see an advertisement for a part-time job that would fit around your current life. All you need to do is apply for it.

Other possibilities are hidden. You have to seek them out by searching for them. Sometimes it takes a lot of work to uncover a concealed possibility. However, these buried opportunities can turn out to be the most worthwhile.

In order to discover opportunities, ask yourself, "What can I do?" and write a list of possibilities in such areas as:

. Learning new skills

. Exercising and Eating Right

. **Earning more money**

Decide which opportunities you'd like to actively pursue. Which ones would you enjoy the most? Don't set your heart on just one or two. At this stage, you won't know which activities you'll be able to do on a long-term basis and which ones won't work out for reasons beyond your control.

Opportunities are worth investigating because they broaden your experience of life and make your life more enjoyable. If you pursue as many opportunities as possible in a variety of different areas, you'll enrich your life and become a more positive person.

What Really Holds Back Financial Freedom?

Procrastination is the killer of many things. You know you should exercise. You know you should study for a test. You know you should prepare healthy meals. You know you should do your laundry before you run out of underwear. But you still put it off to tomorrow, and when tomorrow comes, you put if off again. In fact, you keep putting it off until it becomes a full-fledged emergency.

Most of us do the same thing when it comes to our money. We don't put take our plans for retirement seriously enough. All of us are getting older each day, yet we tell ourselves that the government will take care of us or that we can rely on social security. Often times our fears lead us to ignore the significance of money and our present and future money needs.

All this procrastination stresses us out. We know that if we just did the items on our ever-expanding to-do list before we had to do them, we would live calmer lives, get more done, and perform better on those very things.

So why don't we just do the things we should before they become emergencies? Why do we procrastinate, and is there anything we can do about it?

There are many reasons we procrastinate. Each one of these reasons causes us to procrastinate in different ways, and each reason has its own technique for overcoming it.

One of the reasons we procrastinate around money is because we feel "in over our heads". It's easy for people to feel overwhelmed by money and investing so we pass the task to a "professional advisor." However, financial advisors take our money and generate thousands of dollars in yearly fees in the process. When we take control of our money by getting a financial education and buying stocks directly, we eliminate unnecessary fees and increase our profits. We also eliminate financial stress and give ourselves peace of mind.

Forgetfulness is another main reason why people procrastinate. We mistakenly think that we can remember to do everything. However, while we may be able to remember to do the dishes, the laundry, walk the dog, etc., we then forget to file our taxes. This is unintentional procrastination. We have every intention of doing the task, but the time comes and goes, and we simply forget. However, we simply can't forget about our financial future. It's too important. For procrastination caused by forgetfulness, making a to-do list can help.

Get in the habit of taking action.

Set financial goals.

Don't wait.

The longer you put off getting a financial education and investing in the stock market, the more opportunities you will miss. As I've often said, the companies that are creating some of the cutting-edge technology we use today are often publically traded. Shareholders have earned millions over the past ten years alone because the share price of some of these companies has increased dramatically. Instead of just being a user of technology you can be an investor.

The solution to achieving financial freedom lies in taking ***action***.

Those who make a plan, win.

So set financial goals. <u>Decide what you want your life to look like one year from today.</u>

Learn how to sell covered calls for monthly income. <u>Decide you're going to earn $5,000 per month.</u>

Now go make great thing happen.

You deserve to have financial freedom and be a wealthy investor.

The Wealthy Investor program is here to support you.

The Wealthy Investor Program

When the world changes, the companies we want to own should change.

Tyrone Jackson, The Wealthy Investor, says, "The Wealthy Investor Program is for those who want to change their lives by getting the education they didn't get in high school or even college. In today's world, to be successful you need that financial education."

Over the past few years the stock market has produced enormous amounts of wealth. Those who have a financial education and invest in the right stocks control their financial destiny.

In The Wealthy Investor program I teach three major strategies:

Covered Call Writing
Covered call writing allows any investor to generate monthly residual income.

Dividend Capturing
Institutional investors collect millions of dollars per quarter

collecting dividends on Dow components like McDonalds, NIKE and AT&T. So can you.

Volatility Trading

Volatility trading can be defined as the rapid changing of a stock price. If you pick the right stocks, it is possible to buy and sell the shares over and over.

As stock prices change throughout the day, you're making money while you are out enjoying your life.

My hope is that you will allow me to be your teacher, guide and mentor. With that said, perhaps you can become one of my best and most successful students.

Join me now at **www.TheWealthyInvestor.net**

The Wealthy Investor Resource Guide

In my products and services, I share with you my favorite stock trades and long-term investments. Here are a few Wealthy Investor Resources you may want to take advantage of:

The Wealthy Investor's Guide to Stock Market Success
This easy to follow audio program will teach you the basics of trading and investing.

www.TheWealthyInvestor.net/guidetostockmarketsuccess/

Hot Stocks Big Profits
Follow Tyrone's stock picks for long-term investing and wealth building.

www.TheWealthyInvestor.net/hotstocksbigprofits/

Volatility 2.0
This special report will show you step by step how to earn consistent profits by volatility trading in a bull market.

www.TheWealthyInvestor.net/volatility20/

In *Trading Stocks Made Easy: How Anyone Can Create Financial Freedom in the Stock Market*, Tyrone Jackson introduces you to the Wealthy Investor principles that debunk the idea that todays market is complex and out of reach to the everyday investor.

In easy to understand language, you will learn:

- What makes a stock price rise
- How to increase your dividend income
- How to start selling covered calls for monthly income

Before you pay a financial advisor to manage your money, let Tyrone Jackson give you the financial education you need to prosper as a self-directed investor.

You can follow Mr. Jackson's weekly trades at www.witradeschool.com

A frequent guest on radio and television, **Tyrone Jackson** (aka The Wealthy Investor) helps his students earn thousands of dollars per month, trading and investing in the stock market.

"I have to give tremendous props to Tyrone on being able to communicate his strategies and help people not only construct a plan to trade for cash flow, but a plan to build lasting wealth for the long term." - *Ka P.*

"Tyrone's wide-ranging understanding of the financial markets, along with his genuine care for the people he works with, have changed my mindset about money, and subsequently changed my life."- *Valencia Y.*

Made in the USA
Monee, IL
04 November 2026

67380499R00066